THIS IS YOUR MOMENT TO *RUN*

GO & TELL

SHAWN BRANN

COMPANION WORKBOOK

for individuals, churches, and small groups

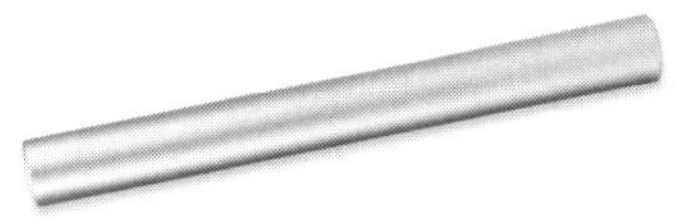

GO & TELL—THIS IS YOUR MOMENT TO RUN

Any text formatting (bold, italics, underlines) in Scripture quotations are added by the author for emphasis.

Details in some anecdotes and stories have been changed to protect the identities of persons mentioned.

Trade paperback ISBN 978-0-9822876-3-7

Cover design and layout by Micah Conger. Edited by Allison Griffin.

Published in Dallas, Texas, by Zürich House Publishing.

Zürich House Publishing
P.O. Box 92366
Southlake, TX 76092 (USA)
www.zurichhousepublishing.com

Printed in the United States of America
1 2 3 4 5 6 7 8 9 10

CONTENTS

1

BC to AD—EXCUSES STINK

> "Jesus said: 'A certain man was preparing a great banquet and invited many guests. At the time of the banquet he sent his servant to tell those who had been invited, "Come, for everything is now ready." But they all alike began to make excuses.'" Luke 14:16–18

Excuses are like garbage cans. We all have them, and they all stink. Do you remember when God called Moses to be his spokesmen to Pharaoh in Exodus 4? Moses responded, "O Lord, I have never been eloquent, neither in the past nor since you have spoken to your servant. I am slow of speech and tongue." (4:10) God basically responds by telling Moses his excuse stunk: "Who gave man his mouth? Who makes him deaf or mute? Who gives him sight or makes him blind? Is it not I, the LORD? Now go; I will help you speak and will teach you what to say." (4:11–12) And, how did Moses respond? "O Lord, please send someone else to do it." (4:13) God was not happy with Moses' excuses. Like Moses, God has also called you to Go & Tell his message. There should be no reason for excuses. They stink to God.

CONTEMPLATE

1. When you hear of Jesus as a king, what goes through your mind? Does this description give the impression of a ruthless dictator in your mind, a loving king who is sovereign in his authority and eternal reign, or something else? Why?

2. Is anything taking your attention away from Christ? Like Leonardo da Vinci did with his paintbrush, how can you refocus your attention and adoration back to Jesus?

3. When you read the content under "Caesar, Jesus, and Good News," how would you articulate—in a few words—what the gospel is?

4. When we encounter King Jesus, what are the two responses we should have?

5. The Gospel Baton, the message we have been given as believers to share, has been handed down through the ages. What benefits, opportunities, and expectations come with it?

RESPOND

Throughout your day, write down descriptions of who Jesus is and why his message is important to everyone around you. Picture yourself as a spiritual runner, with the Gospel Baton in your hand.

APPLY

Write a list of people you know who need to hear the gospel message. We will come back to this list throughout this workbook, add to it, pray over them, and be prepared for the gospel to be given to them.

....

....

....

....

....

....

....

....

LISTEN

What is the Holy Spirit saying to you?

....

....

....

....

....

....

....

....

....

"I am the way, the truth and the life." – Jesus

2

THE FIRST CENTURY—JUST ASK

> "But you will receive power when the Holy Spirit comes on you; and you will be my witnesses in Jerusalem, and in all Judea and Samaria, and to the ends of the earth." Acts 1:8

To share the gospel without the Holy Spirit on you and in you is as frightening and disastrous as skydiving without a parachute. To state the obvious, it won't end well. So, how are you filled with Holy Spirit? It's quite simple. Just as you receive salvation, you also receive the Holy Spirit. In Luke 11:13, Jesus said, "If you then, being evil, know how to give good gifts to your children, how much more will your heavenly Father give the Holy Spirit to those who ask him!" That's the answer. All you have to do is ask. And, just like salvation, whether you feel anything or not, you receive the Holy Spirit. Then jump out of your comfort zone, and watch how he carries you along as you share the gospel with those around you.

Baton Carriers: The first disciples, Mary, Martha, Stephen, Paul, Clement of Rome, Ignatius of Antioch

CONTEMPLATE

1. Have you or anyone you know referenced the Holy Spirit as an "it" instead of God, the third person of the trinity? Why do you think this is the case?

....

....

....

2. If someone asked you, "Where does God live?" what would you say? Why?

....

....

....

3. Have you ever tried to evangelize without the Holy Spirit? What were the results?

....

....

....

4. When the Holy Spirit lives in you, how does he help you share the good news of Jesus? And, what symbolic ways does he help you in your everyday life and calling?

....

....

....

5. Is your life like a motorboat or a sailboat? Are there areas of your life you haven't fully given to God so he can work out his perfect will for you? If so, what are they and what will you do about it?

....

....

....

RESPOND

When Paul closed his letter in 2 Corinthians 13:14, he wrote, "May the grace of the Lord Jesus Christ, and the love of God, and the fellowship of the Holy Spirit be with you all." Every day and throughout the day, have fellowship with the Holy Spirit. Make him your best friend, learn to hear his voice, feel what he feels, and walk with him step by step. Watch how he radically transforms your life and uses you in ways you never thought were possible.

APPLY

Are you uncertain that you are filled with the Holy Spirit and have a relationship with him? If so, take a moment and focus your attention on your Heavenly Father. As his child, simply ask, "Father, will you give me the Holy Spirit?" You can be sure that your heavenly father will give you this wonderful gift. Now, begins the greatest and most valuable resource and relationship necessary for fulfilling your life's calling and effective evangelism. Write down the date of this monumental moment.

....

....

....

....

....

LISTEN

What is the Holy Spirit saying to you?

....

....

....

....

....

"Without the Spirit of God, we can do nothing. We are as ships without wind. We are useless." –C.H. Spurgeon

3

THE 100s–TALKING WITH JESUS

> "And pray in the Spirit on all occasions with all kinds of prayers and requests." Ephesians 6:18

Did you know that praying is a fancy word for "communicating" with God. My wife and I communicate with each other every day, throughout the day. Sometimes we sit down for long conversations, other times we express ourselves with non-verbal communication. We are honest with each other. We share our joys, our disappointments, our requests, questions, and our victories. We don't try to impress each other with big words or speak with a special tone of voice. She knows me, and I know her. There's no need to impress. So it is with our conversations with God. He knows you. Talk to him. Listen to him. Communicate with him often; talk with him about everything. Grow intimate with him and know his voice better than any other that may be heard throughout your day.

Baton Carriers: Justin Martyr, Tatian, Theophilus of Antioch, Irenaeus, Tertullian

CONTEMPLATE

1. What does the word "preach" mean now that you know the background of the Greek word *kerusso*? How does this change your view on sharing the gospel and living out your Christian faith?

2. Do you spend enough time in prayer to hear God's voice over all the other voices around you? If not, what will you do about it?

3. How did Charles Spurgeon compare prayer to a boat?

4. We must pray, and we must preach. Is this balanced in your life? Which do you tend to lean more toward?

5. Under the subtitle, "But, I Don't Have Time to Pray," what can we learn from Billy Graham's interview?

RESPOND

There is power in prayer. Take a moment and pray for the salvation of the names you listed from Chapter One. Ask God how you can be involved in bringing the gospel to them.

APPLY

Jesus had private places where he would get away to and pray. Do you have a special prayer location? If not, take this week to consider where that special place could be, and set it as a special place where you and God meet. This could be a private room, a specific chair, a unique spot by a river, etc. Write down where that place is, and ask the Holy Spirit to meet you there.

....

....

....

....

....

....

....

....

LISTEN

What is the Holy Spirit saying to you?

....

....

....

....

....

....

....

"A prayerless Christian is a powerless Christian." –Billy Graham

4

THE 200s–TO ALL, BY ALL

> "Everyone who calls on the name of the Lord will be saved." Romans 10:13

It was 1973. Every seat in the stadium in Johannesburg, Africa was filled. The gospel message was being proclaimed by evangelist Billy Graham. As the crowd sat on the edge of their seats, Graham delivered this famous line, "Christianity is not a white man's religion. And don't ever let anybody tell you that it's white or black. Christ belongs to all people! He belongs to the whole world." Those words still ring true today. Jesus Christ and his gospel are relevant and belong to every person in the cosmoses of your life. The gospel belongs to all people and all people are called to share the gospel. Billy Graham took the Gospel Baton and shared the good news around the world. Now, it's in your hand. Will you take it to your cosmos, too?

Baton Carriers: Countless martyrs during Roman Persecutions, Hippolytus of Rome, Origen of Alexandria, Cyprian, Constantine

CONTEMPLATE

1. What is the difference between the Greek words *ethnos* and *cosmos*?

2. Why do many people only equate taking the gospel to the "world" as being a missionary overseas?

3. Are there only certain people God calls to share his gospel, or is everyone, including you, expected to evangelize? Is everyone at your church sharing the gospel? If not, what can you do to encourage those in leadership to get everyone involved in evangelism?

4. In the last sentence of the section titled "Your Mission Field," we are told that God chooses to partner with us in getting his gospel to the world. Are you living in a way that God is glad to partner with you, or is there more you can do in partnering with him for the advancement of his gospel?

5. We are called to go into the different systems, cosmoses, of our world and share the gospel. What cosmoses are you part of?

RESPOND

Of all the billions of people in the world, God has chosen you to be his spokesman in the different cosmoses you are a part of. From now on, when you walk into your work, school, or family gatherings, don't see yourself as just an employee, student, or family member, but as God's chosen ambassador. God has put the advancement of his gospel into your hands for those around you. You've got this!

APPLY

Ask the Holy Spirit to reveal the cosmoses that you may be part of without ever realizing it. Write them down along with a couple of people in each who need Jesus. Add them to your list from Chapter One.

LISTEN

What is the Holy Spirit saying to you?

"Do all the good you can, by all the means you can, in all the places you can, at all the times you can, to all the people you can, as long as ever you can." –John Wesley

5

THE 300s–HOTI

> "And a great crowd of people followed him because they saw the miraculous signs he had preformed on the sick." John 6:2

Can you imagine what it must have been like to hang out with Jesus? Almost everywhere he went, there was a crowd. He was the center of life and activity across the entire country during his ministry. He had people in every village buzzing with his name and message on their tongues as many left to follow him across the country. And, why did they continuously follow Jesus from town to town? John tells us, "... because they saw the miraculous signs." (John 6:2) The Greek word for "because" is *hoti*. This is a conjunction word. They followed Jesus. Why? Because of the miracles. Now the Gospel Baton has been handed to us. In Matthew 10:8, Jesus tells us to do the same. Miracles are a sure way to get people's attention and for them to potentially follow Jesus.

Baton Carriers: Athanasius, Ulfilas,
Martin of Tours, Ambrose of Milan, John Chrysostom

CONTEMPLATE

1. Did you know God wants to work miracles through you just like he did for those in the Bible or well-known believers over the centuries?

2. What keeps you from praying for the sick or believing God for miracles?

3. Why do you think not everyone gets healed? How does this affect your attitude when you are prompted to pray for someone?

4. Have you seen or heard of people faking miracles? If so, has it caused you to become a skeptic regarding miracles? Ask the Holy Spirit to begin to build your trust back and believe in miracles again.

5. Are miracles a result of your great faith? And, what happens if you don't see the miracles you hope to experience? Do you quit praying for miracles or keep believing?

RESPOND

Have you ever been used by God in the healing of a sick, injured, or those with a physical handicap? How did it make you feel? If not, begin to ask the Holy Spirit to point out people around you who need prayer. Step out in faith, and see what God does. Whether someone gets visibly healed or not, they will for sure be ministered to and feel loved.

APPLY

When praying for the sick or the demon possessed, remember the victory of their healing or deliverance was won through Christ. Therefore, speak life or freedom to individuals instead of begging God. His Gospel Baton is in your hands, and the Holy Spirit is within you. You have been given the authority. Write down the names of those in need of a miracle, and begin declaring victory over them. Come back to this list in the next days or weeks to see how God has responded.

....

....

....

....

....

....

LISTEN

What is the Holy Spirit saying to you?

....

....

....

....

....

....

"When Jesus died on the cross and cried out, 'It is finished!,' he not only died for our sins, but for our diseases too." –Kathryn Kuhlman

6

THE 400s–JESUS GETS IT

> "He made Him who knew no sin to be sin for us, that we might become the righteousness of God in Him." 2 Corinthians 5:21

The greatest injustice ever done to any individual in history was the mistreatment of Jesus. Imagine. Jesus was perfect; he did nothing wrong. But, he choose to take on the sins and punishments of the entire world—including yours and mine! We just saw how he healed all, loved all, and brought joy to every city he entered. He was, and is, good news. Yet, he was arrested, beaten, tortured, and crucified. To make matters worse, when he died on the cross, he was alone. He was forsaken by all. Jesus could have decided that he would only have sympathy for us. Instead, he choose to identify with us by taking every injustice imaginable upon himself. If there is anyone who understands having an injustice done to them, it's the very one we follow. He gets it. And, he can help anyone through it.

Baton Carriers: Jerome, Augustine of Hippo, John Cassian, Ninian, Clovis of France

CONTEMPLATE

1. Are there some injustices that have been done to you, like Patrick of Ireland, that God can use for the advancement of his kingdom? What is a simple first step you can take to begin seeing this happen?

2. How much power do Satan and his demons have? What is one of the main ways he tries to defeat a believer?

3. How do bitterness and unforgiveness affect the life of a believer and the advancement of the gospel?

4. Do you find yourself believing the lies of the enemy or the negative words of others regarding your identity? Why is it sometimes easier to believe those lies than the truth of how God sees you as a follower of Christ?

5. Joy. Joy. Joy. An incredible gift God has given us is the ability to have joy in the midst of suffering. Do you need joy today? What are three things God has done for you that are exponentially greater than the current problems you are facing? Let those things bring you joy today!

RESPOND

Have you been wronged? Are you still holding unforgiveness or bitterness in your heart because of it? With your eyes closed, picture God right in front of you. Now, hand that offense or person to him. Walk away determined to never let that be a roadblock to the purpose he has for you.

APPLY

Go through the Bible or search Bible verses that speak of who you are. Write down ten descriptions with the corresponding verses on small cards and put them throughout your home, car, office, etc. Remind yourself daily of your identity in Christ. Here's a start. I am … 1. Loved—"For God so loved the world that he gave his only Son that whoever will believe in him will not perish but have eternal life." (John 3:16)

....

....

....

....

....

LISTEN

What is the Holy Spirit saying to you?

....

....

....

....

....

....

....

"Christ knows His own sheep 'by name.' There are no unknown Christians, no insignificant sons of God … The faceless man has a face, the nameless man a name, when Jesus picks him out of the multitude and calls him to Himself." –A.W. Tozer

7

THE 500s–MORE VALUABLE THAN THE SUN

> "For we are God's handiwork, created in Christ Jesus to do good works, which God prepared in advance for us to do." Ephesians 2:10

God has given you talents and creativity to use for the advancement of his gospel. Use them. John Chrysostom was one of the early leaders in the church in the fourth century. He used his talent of speaking and combined it with creativity. He became so effective that he was given the nickname, "Golden-mouthed." As a result, the gospel message exploded around Constantinople. It was said about him that, "It were better that the sun should cease to shine, than that his mouth should be shut." Can the same be said about the way you are combining creativitiy and your talents for the good news of Jesus to get out? Are you more valuable than the sun to those around you?

Baton Carriers: Benedict of Nursia, Columba, Columbanus, Gregory, Bertha of Kent

CONTEMPLATE

1. Look around you. What are some amazing creations you see? How does God continue to reveal his creative wonders to us daily?

.....

.....

.....

2. Are you a voice or an echo? Are you comparing yourself to others, or are you keeping your eyes on Christ?

.....

.....

.....

3. Have you ever tried to build something for God when he wasn't asking it of you? How can you run with the Gospel Baton while being faithful to what he's called you to do?

.....

.....

.....

4. What are some of the ways Jesus was creative in getting his gospel to the masses or individuals?

.....

.....

.....

.....

5. What are some creative ideas you've seen others use for the advancement of the gospel?

.....

.....

.....

.....

RESPOND

Determine to be creative. Begin asking "Why?" in regards to how you are living and sharing your faith. Let the Holy Spirit help you think outside of the box and be more effective in advancing his kingdom.

APPLY

First take a moment and pray for those unbelievers you listed in Chapter One. Next, ask the Holy Spirit for a creative way to share his gospel with those unbelievers. What is he saying to you? Write it down and put actions to his response. You'll be surprised how God can use it for the advancement of his kingdom.

LISTEN

What is the Holy Spirit saying to you?

"The Christian is the one whose imagination should fly beyond the stars." –Francis Schaeffer

8

THE 600s–A SMOOTH SAVIOR

> "They said to the woman, 'We no longer believe just because of what you said; now we have heard for ourselves, and we know that this man really is the Savior of the world.'" John 4:42

When it came to sharing the gospel, Jesus was smooth. Before the woman at the well shared her testimony, Jesus shared his. Of course, his was a bit different, with no A, B, or C. He *is* the testimony. But, there are some things we can learn from the way Jesus shared the gospel too. Go back and read the story in John 4 after becoming aware of these three cultural things: 1. People typically carried their own portable water buckets. 2. Jews wouldn't talk to Samaritans. 3. Men would often withdraw a distance of at least twenty feet from women of another region to be culturally or socially acceptable. Here's one thing you may now notice. By deliberately sitting on the well without a bucket, Jesus placed himself strategically to be in need of the lady. This was not a coincidence of their meeting but a divine setup.

Baton Carriers: Isidore of Seville, Edwin of Northumbria, John of Bergamo, Willibrord of Northumbria, Bede the Venerable

CONTEMPLATE

1. What were some strategic ways Jesus shared the gospel (his testimony) to the woman at the well? What are some lessons we can learn from Jesus in this story?

....

....

....

2. What are the ABCs of a testimony?

....

....

....

3. God wants to give you divine encounters to share the gospel. Are you ready? If not, what do you need to do to be ready?

....

....

....

4. In the chapter, you read about how Larry Tomczak has his testimony printed and gives them out everywhere he goes. What can you do to get your testimony to those you meet?

....

....

....

....

5. What is the one-two punch, and how can you utilize it while running with the Gospel Baton?

....

....

....

....

RESPOND

After preparing your testimony, ask the Holy Spirit to give you divine appointments. Be alert and expectant for him to answer. And, when he does, be faithful to respond. This could be the beginning of a fruitful evangelistic lifestyle!

APPLY

Write out your testimony. Remember to keep it short and possibly use this three-point outline to stay focused: 1. Pre-salvation life 2. Salvation 3. How your life is now since following Christ

....

....

....

....

....

....

....

....

LISTEN

What is the Holy Spirit saying to you?

....

....

....

....

....

....

....

....

"God has ordered your steps to touch the life of someone so that you share your testimony." –Kenneth Ulmer

9

THE 700s–GET DIRTY

> "Therefore, prepare your minds for action, keep sober in spirit, set your hope completely on the grace to be brought to you at the revelation of Jesus Christ." 1 Peter 1:13

If the Bible were a movie, perhaps it could be categorized under the Action genre. The entire book is loaded with stories of men, women, and a God who were constantly taking action. Starting with God creating the world, through the exodus, the kings, prophets speaking of a coming king, the Messiah coming, the disciples sharing the gospel, and the last chapter of Jesus' return, every page is packed with action. All the stories weren't perfect, tidy, and clean. It reminds me of Proverbs 14:4 that says, "Without oxen a stable stays clean, but you need a strong ox for a large harvest." When we do nothing for the gospel, our lives are tidy and clean. But, action is where the story happens. You may get dirty. But it's all part of the exciting adventure of running with the Gospel Baton in hand.

Baton Carriers: Lioba, Alcuin,Charlemagne

CONTEMPLATE

1. We have to "Tell," but we first must ... what?

2. Under the section "God Goes with Goers," what can we learn from Genesis 1:2–3 and the power of the spoken word?

3. We are to Tell, but first we have to Go. Why is the first step toward sharing the gospel sometimes the hardest?

4. Have you ever shared the gospel and walked away thinking that you failed? How can times that seem like failure actually work to advance the gospel?

5. Have you been dreaming of how God can use you for his kingdom? What areas of your life can you move from dreaming to actually doing?

RESPOND

Pray for those on your list from Chapter One to hear the gospel.

APPLY

Write down a couple ways you can take action to see the gospel brought to those on your Chapter One list. This may include taking them to your church, out for coffee with the intention of sharing the gospel, or something different.

LISTEN

What is the Holy Spirit saying to you?

"Never pity missionaries; envy them. They are where the real actions is–where life and death, sin and grace, Heaven and Hell converge." –Robert Shannon

10

THE 800s–YOU NEED BOTH

> "Above all, love each other deeply, because love covers over a multitude of sins." 1 Peter 4:8

The combination of truth and love was, and still is, among one of the most powerful causes of the advancement of the gospel. In describing the first-century of Gospel Baton runners to the Roman Emperor Hadrian, Aristides said, "They love one another. They never fail to help widows, they save orphans from those who will hurt them. If they have something, they give freely to the man who has nothing; if they see a stranger, they take him home and are happy, as though he were a real brother." When we share the truth of the gospel without loving others; we give facts but in a way where no one hears it. But if we only love without sharing the gospel, it's deceptive; we are essentially supporting and affirming unbelievers while keeping them in denial of their sin. Give truth, but make sure you give it with the same measure of love.

Baton Carriers: Ansgar, King Alfred

CONTEMPLATE

1. Have you ever experienced someone preaching in a public square or street corner and sensed condemnation instead of love? If you were an unbeliever, how would that make you feel?

....

....

....

2. Would you consider yourself more of a lion or a lamb in your approach with the gospel? How can you become more balanced?

....

....

....

3. Do you also find it hardest to share your faith with those closest to you? If so, why is this? And, how can you overcome this challenge?

....

....

....

....

4. How can our physical bodies be a reminder of consciously loving those around us as mentioned under the section "We All Need to Be Loved"?

....

....

....

5. Why is love so important in sharing the gospel? How did Jesus show love to those around him?

....

....

....

....

RESPOND

Throughout your week, ask the Holy Spirit to show you what you would look like, as Ossa did with Eugene Peterson, if all the love left you. Get this image in your head. Determine in your heart to never live a without love.

APPLY

In I Corinthians 13:4–13, Paul gives a list of what love looks like and does. Write down this list. Then go through the list and ask the Holy Spirit to show you where you need improvement. Ask him to help you.

....

....

....

....

....

....

....

....

LISTEN

What is the Holy Spirit saying to you?

....

....

....

....

....

....

....

....

....

"It's not about how much you do, but how much love you put into what you do that counts." –Mother Teresa

11

THE 900s–LIVING AND ACTIVE SEEDS

"The word of God is living and active." Hebrews 4:12

Seeds. They aren't the most exciting things to look at or talk about. But the power of a seed is astonishing—especially the seed of the gospel. Have you ever thought about this amazing seed? Look again what the Bible says in Hebrews 4:12, and remember that the gospel is the word of God. First, the seed of the gospel is alive. The gospel isn't just a good story. It is a living message, backed by a living God. And, secondly, it is active. It is always working. Next time you go to share the gospel, think about the power of the seed you are planting in the heart of the one you're telling. The seed may take root immediately; it may take years to germinate. But either way, the person receiving it will never be the same.

Baton Carriers: All the believers whose names and stories are unknown to man but known to God.

CONTEMPLATE

1. Sharing the gospel is like sowing seeds. Have you been sowing the gospel message?

2. Where are you the most effective: planting the message, watering what others have planted, or reaping? How can you work on your weaknesses and improve on your strengths?

3. You read the list of those who sowed seeds that eventually led to the salvation of Billy Graham. Can you make a list of those who sowed seeds that led to your salvation? Try to write it out.

4. At the end of your life, will you be commended by God because of how famous you became or by how faithful you were? Why does our culture celebrate being famous more than faithful?

5. Jesus lived as a man who was urgent. How can you make the urgency of the gospel more real in your daily life?

RESPOND

You were challenged to see yourself as God's ambassador in Chapter Four. This week, see yourself also as God's farmer. Every time you share the good news of Jesus, you plant a living seed. You may not see the harvest, but you can be assured that the gospel was sown!

APPLY

Write down a strategy for how your church can celebrate the process of evangelism and those involved. How can you celebrate those who plant the gospel, those who water the gospel, and those who reap the harvest? Take this strategy to the leaders of your church, and trust God to use it according to his purposes.

LISTEN

What is the Holy Spirit saying to you?

"You take care of the sowing, and God will take care of the growing." –Unknown

12

THE 1000s–BE A STAR

> "After Jesus was born in Bethlehem in Judea, during the time of King Herod, Magi from the east came to Jerusalem and asked, "Where is the one who has been born king of the Jews? We saw his star in the east and have come to worship him." Matthew 2:1–2

Astronomers say that the light given off by closest star to Earth (besides the sun) would take over four years to reach our eyes. Have you ever considered that fact in light of the star from the Christmas story? That star had one purpose: to tell the magi that Jesus was alive and point them to him. That's exactly what happened. This was no coincidence. Years before Jesus was born, God strategically had the light of that one star shine because he knew that there would be some wise men who would be looking into the sky, see the light emitted years later, and follow it to Jesus. Is it possible that before you were born, God also determined to place you where you are so you not only to find him, but also to be like that star to those around you—to tell of the good news of Jesus and led them to him?

Baton Carriers: Vladimir, Anselm of Aosta, Stanislaus of Krakow

CONTEMPLATE

1. Have you ever had one of those "construction worker" moments? What was it?

2. Look under the section, "Your Life Is Strategically Planned." What two areas of your life have been predetermined according to Acts 17?

3. What is the purpose of God determining where you live and when?

4. Have you ever met someone you thought was too far gone to be reached with the gospel? Why?

5. To effectively share the gospel, we need to have spiritual eyes and ears that do ... what?

RESPOND

We talk about how no one is too lost. This includes those on your list from Chapter One. God has strategically set them up to know him. It is highly probable that you are that "construction worker" in their life. Let your light shine.

APPLY

Write down your dream place to live. Next write down your ideal time period in world history to be alive. Are they today and right where you are? This is God's perfect place and time for you to know him. Give thanks to God for positioning you to find him. Any other time or place would have been less likely than right here and now.

LISTEN

What is the Holy Spirit saying to you?

"Every divine appointment is preceded by a season of preparation." –Mark Batterson

13

THE 1100s–MAKE A LIFE, NOT JUST A LIVING

> "...let your light shine before others, that they may see your good deeds and glorify your Father in heaven." Matthew 5:16

In many cultures, the topic of money topic is off-limits. In this chapter, you read that Jesus talked about money more than faith and prayer combined. Did you know that money is mentioned in the Bible over eight hundred times? Money has to be talked about because how we use it matters. An old adage says that we make a living by what we get, but we make a life by what we give. Living a generous life should be a characteristic of every believer. Martin Luther once halfway joked that, "God divided the hand into fingers so that money could slip through." Basically, we are expected to be givers—and not just of money. We are to be givers of money, time, talents, the gospel, and our lives. Giving is a characteristic of God. For God so the loved the world that he gave.

Baton Carriers: Bernard of Clairvaus, the Friars

CONTEMPLATE

1. Why do you think Jesus said that the love of money is the root of all evil? How can money work for or against those who are running with the Gospel Baton?

....

....

....

....

2. Was it surprising to see that Jesus was a philanthropist? How does this change the way you may be able to share the gospel?

....

....

....

3. Why do you think many great ministries and missionaries have abandoned sharing the gospel but have continued to do humanitarian work?

....

....

....

4. Waldo was a great giver. How can you be like Waldo? Are there any ministries you can be more generous to? How can you give more to your local church?

....

....

....

5. What are some other good deeds you can do? This could include social work, medical missions, homeless outreaches, etc.

....

....

....

RESPOND

Ask the Holy Spirit to show you how you can be a better steward of his resources he's entrusted to you for the advancement of the gospel. Be ready for him to speak to you and then be faithful on what he says.

APPLY

Go to the ATM and take out some money to give away. This may be $10, $50, $100, or more. As you go about the day, ask the Holy Spirit to reveal who to give it to and how you can use it to share his gospel. Obey, and be ready for a life to be changed. Come back and write down what happened.

....

....

....

....

....

....

....

....

LISTEN

What is the Holy Spirit saying to you?

....

....

....

....

....

....

....

....

"If a man gets his attitude about money straightened out, then almost all other areas of his life will be straightened out." –Billy Graham

14

THE 1200s–DEFINE YOUR BULLSEYE

"But in your hearts revere Christ as Lord. Always be prepared to give an answer to everyone who asks you to give the reason for the hope that you have. But do this with gentleness and respect." 1 Peter 3:15

Start with the end in mind. Our goal in evangelizing is not to wow someone with our theological knowledge, but to clearly present to them the good news—that Jesus is king and that we can have eternal life because of it. It doesn't matter how eloquent your words are but how clear the message is. Remember in Chapter Three that to preach the gospel is not about delivering some stirring sermon, but rather about speaking on behalf of the king. His desire is to, "seek and to save that which is lost." (Luke 19:10) For, Jesus, "did not come to call the righteous, but sinners to repentance." (Luke 5:32) We have to stay focused on why Jesus came. The first condition of salvation is not knowledge, but meeting Christ. We need to make that the bullseye for everyone who hears our message.

Baton Carriers: Dominic de Guzman, Albertus Magnus, Clare of Assisi, Bonaventure

CONTEMPLATE

1. If you were called upon in the park in Ukraine, would you be ready to share the gospel?

....

....

....

2. What is the KISS principle, and how does it relate to sharing the gospel?

....

....

....

3. What was significant about the Roman soldier's shoes as it relates to evangelism?

....

....

....

4. When you are about to tell an unbeliever about Jesus, do you get nervous? How can being prepared in advance and partnering with the Holy Spirit help?

....

....

....

5. What does "land the plane" mean? Would you be ready to lead someone to Christ if they asked? If not, write down a simple prayer of faith and confession in Christ you could share when that time comes.

....

....

....

....

....

RESPOND

Ask God to help you find the perfect method of sharing his message that fits your life. Memorize it. And then … use it.

APPLY

Research different approaches for making the gospel simple and write them down. Which one are you most comfortable with? Five are mentioned in this chapter. Some other ones include Evangelism Explosion, Steps to Peace with God, G.O.S.P.E.L., Three Circles Evangelism, Gospel Bead Bracelet, the Circle Method, and the Alpha Course Structure to name a few. Google to find more. You may even come up with your own.

....

....

....

....

....

....

....

....

LISTEN

What is the Holy Spirit saying to you?

....

....

....

....

....

"They were meant for the ear and the heart of the sinner, not for professors, or grade books, or classrooms. Before God, the only critic that counted was the man or woman who raised their hand and came forward to receive Christ. All else counted as dung."
–Reinhard Bonnke (on his messages and preaching style)

14

THE 1300s– BREATH, BALLOONS, AND BIBLES

> "All Scripture is God-breathed and is useful for teaching, rebuking, correcting and training in righteousness..." 2 Timothy 3:16

The Bible is God's word, given to us by him. Paul reminds Timothy that scripture is "God-breathed." God emitted his own substance into the Bible. Let me explain: Imagine a balloon. It is formless until one breathes into it. When it is fully inflated, you tie off the end, and the air remains in the balloon. The air formed the balloon and sustains it. And, if you look at the DNA inside, it would be from the breath of the one who blew into it. So it is with the Bible. God breathed into human language, forming the Bible as we have it today. And when we open it, we find that same God is the one sustaining it. His DNA is there. God did not just write the Bible, he is contained inside it. What an inheritance we have. Use it always.

Baton Carriers: John of Monte Corvino, Johann Tauler, Jan Hus

CONTEMPLATE

1. Why is the gospel so offensive to many people?

2. Do you see the unbelievers in your cosmoses as in a house that is on fire mentioned in the story? How does this story make the reality of gospel more urgent?

3. What does it mean to "hide behind the word"?

4. What is the difference between the *rhema* word and the *logos* word?

5. Do you read the Bible daily? Do you memorize verses? If no, determine today to make this a daily habit in your life. Knowing God's Word is paramount in being effective in evangelism.

RESPOND

Once again, pray for the list of unbelievers from Chapter One. Have you had an opportunity to share the gospel with them yet? If not, be prepared for God to make a way for you, or someone else around them, to share with them.

APPLY

Write down a few social issues that are hot topics for you. These are topics that can easily cause you to debate over. How have you responded in the past? Now, write down how you can respond, not with your opinion, but by "hiding behind the word." Start off each topic by writing, "The Bible says ..."

....

....

....

....

....

....

....

....

LISTEN

What is the Holy Spirit saying to you?

....

....

....

....

....

....

....

"We are inheritors, not inventors, of the Bible." –Unknown

16

THE 1400s–HISTORY MAKERS

> "I pray that they will all be one, just as you and I are one—as you are in me, Father, and I am in you. And may they be in us so that the world will believe you sent me." John 17:21

I've found that one of the greatest strategies of the enemy is to cause believers to compete and fight among each other. The last thing Jesus prayed was for the believers to be one. Why? So that "the world will believe" Jesus was sent from God. We are to be united together with Christ, not divided in our own agendas or biblical interpretations. Consider these three approaches to life for a believer and see where you land. Approach One: If life is about you, then you have to be great and everyone else is your competition. Approach Two: If life is about making a difference, then your church or ministry has to be great and other churches or ministries will be your competition. Approach Three: If life is about making history, then God is great and the devil is your competition. The Gospel Baton has always been most effective when in the hands of history makers!

Baton Carriers: Nicholas Hereford, Thomas à Kempis, Johann Gutenberg, Desiderius Erasmus, Albert Durer

CONTEMPLATE

1. Why do you think believers fight with those outside of their denomination? How does this inhibit the gospel from getting to the lost?

2. What could have been the stories of so many believers over the centuries if they had focused on the gospel and not fighting amongst each other? What other countries, like China, may be dramatically different today had believers made the gospel the main focus?

3. The gospel is just like a what? All we have to do is open the cage, let it out, and it will do ... what?

4. What are some peripheral joys that unbelievers have while searching for the ultimate meaning of life?

5. How are we to be like cows in regards to the Scriptures?

RESPOND

Have you quarreled with brothers or sisters in the faith recently? Did it cause division among you? If so, take a moment and ask for God's forgiveness. You may even need to go to them and ask their forgiveness as well. Don't let this minor dispute keep you from fulfilling your purpose.

APPLY

We talked about peripheral questions we have as believers. Many times, these questions hinder us from sharing the gospel. Write down some of these questions you have. Bring those questions to God, and tell him that whether he gives you the answer or not, you will walk by faith that he has a purpose. These questions won't keep you from faithfully running with the Gospel Baton.

....

....

....

....

....

....

....

....

LISTEN

What is the Holy Spirit saying to you?

....

....

....

....

....

....

"Division in the Church is worse than war." –Constantine

17

THE 1500s–BUILDING BOLDNESS

> "The Lord is my light and my salvation–whom shall I fear? The Lord is the stronghold of my life–of whom shall I be afraid?" Psalm 27:1

When I was in my twenties, I needed money for a ministry I had started. So, I accepted a contracted position for the local city's Information Technology department, creating an inventory system for them. It became immediately clear that God had placed me there, not only to make money, but to share the gospel with the dozens of men on my team. As I rode around in the trucks with the men, I made it my goal to share the gospel. Excuses would flood my mind about why that specific ride was a bad time to share Jesus. But, I pressed on. When my contract was up, I had shared the gospel to everyone in the department. I learned that boldness can be built. After each time I shared the gospel, it became easier for me to share with the next person. By the time the last person on my team heard the gospel from me, I was bold like a lion.

Baton Carriers: John Knox, John Calvin,
Anne Askew, Joan Mathurin, Anabaptists

CONTEMPLATE

1. What is the most repeated phrase in the Bible? How does this phrase bring comfort to you when sharing the gospel?

2. When it comes to sharing Jesus, often our hearts say one thing and our heads another. Why is this the case as mentioned under the section "The Evangelism Formula"?

3. Did you know that you had such a rich inheritance of bold believers in your past? How does that give you courage today?

4. If you were to open the mouth of Satan, he would have no what? Why then do we get so afraid of his roars?

5. How can you bring encouragement and courage to other believers?

RESPOND

As a carrier of the Gospel Baton, you come from a bold lineage of believers. Don't let the enemy or your mind make you afraid of what others around you have to say. Look at yourself in the mirror, and remind yourself of your inheritance. You are bold. You are brave. This is who you are in Christ Jesus!

APPLY

Write down the top five things you are afraid of. Do these things keep you from sharing the gospel? If so, ask God to remove all fear and replace it with courage. Now use that courage and begin to share Jesus with the people you listed in Chapter One (and to others around you). God is with you!

LISTEN

What is the Holy Spirit saying to you?

"I am not moved by what I see, I am not moved by what I feel. I am moved by what I believe." –Smith Wigglesworth

18

THE 1600s–TRAIN HARD, FIGHT EASY

> "Have nothing to do with godless myths and old wives' tales; rather, train yourself to be godly." 1 Timothy 4:7

We read that a saint is one who is holy. I love to remind people that the secret to being a saint is to be a saint in secret. Your true character reveals itself when no one is looking. My wife has a saying. It's a military principle, but it can apply for our lives as believers. "Train hard, fight easy." Essentially, the way we train is how we fight. If we train in holiness when no one is looking, then when the temptations or excuses of this world come our way, we have the strength to overcome. But, if we don't train ourselves, it's easy to be weak and fall. Train hard, fight easy, and cross your finish line ready to pass off the Gospel Baton further along in the race than where you got it.

Baton Carriers: Samuel Rutherford, John Owen, John Bunyon, Pastor Philipp Jakob Spener, August Hermann Francke

CONTEMPLATE

1. When you hear the word "holy" what do you think about? What does it actually mean?

2. What does it mean to be in the world but not for the world to be in you?

3. As a believer, the Bible often calls us "saints." What does the word saint mean?

4. When a believer lives a life of sin and gets caught, how does it negatively affect the advancement of the gospel?

5. How can we disqualify ourselves in this race and even shipwreck our faith? When we are tempted, are we sinners? If not, what then makes us sinners?

RESPOND

We live in a time when people claim that living contrary to God's holy word is OK and that God is OK with it. Take a few moments and ask God to convict the heart of the sinner and to reveal his holiness to them.

APPLY

You are in a race, with the Gospel Baton in hand. Hebrews 12:1 says for us to "throw off everything that hinders and the sin that so easily entangles and run with perseverance the race marked out for us." Write down the things that hinder you or the sins that are entangled around you. Confess them to God. Confess them to others. Be free and run! You were born for such a time as this.

LISTEN

What is the Holy Spirit saying to you?

"It is not great talents God blesses so much as great likeness to Jesus." –Robert Murray M'Cheyne

19

THE 1700s–PASSION BREEDS PASSION

"They asked each other, 'Were not our hearts burning within us while he talked with us on the road and opened the Scriptures to us?'" Luke 24:32

We've all lit a fire. You take a match or piece of wood that is on fire and put it on another piece of wood that is not. The two become inflamed. Pretty simple. Did you know that passion, expressed through the power of the Holy Spirit, is much like this? Passion is contagious. The best way to get others passionate for what you believe is to first be passionate yourself. Remember when Jesus was walking on the road to Emmaus after his resurrection? Two women were walking along the rode when Jesus started walking with them. They didn't notice that it was Jesus, but were drawn to his passion. As they looked back on the incident the following day, after realizing that it was Jesus, they both remarked how "their hearts burned within them" as Jesus spoke the Scriptures to them.

Baton Carriers: William Tennent, Jonathan Edwards, David Brainerd, Richard Allen, William Carey

CONTEMPLATE

1. How is passion attractive in sharing the gospel and what could that look like in your life?

2. Would you ever buy a product you knew little about from a salesman who had no passion for the product? Why do you think many unpassionate believers who share Jesus think unbelievers would respond differently?

3. In order to have passion, you don't need the right personality but rather who living in you?

4. What did John Wesley say was his secret for why so many people came to hear him preach?

5. To be passionate, do you have to be overly expressive and charismatic, or can someone have a conservative personality yet exude passion?

RESPOND

Let the prayer of Jim Elliot, the martyred missionary mentioned in Chapter Twenty One, be your prayer throughout the week. "God, I pray, light these idle sticks of my life and may I burn for you."

APPLY

Write down the names of three people you know who have a genuine passion for Jesus. How does their passion for Jesus affect their witness to unbelievers? Ask the Holy Spirit to give you the same fire. And, if possible, let those three individuals know how thankful you are for their example for all believers to follow.

....

....

....

....

....

....

....

....

LISTEN

What is the Holy Spirit saying to you?

....

....

....

....

....

....

....

"The secret of the Christian's passion is simple: Everything we do in life we do it as to the Lord and not to men." –David Jeremiah

20

THE 1800s–GET YOUR OWN T-SHIRT

> "Elisha then picked up Elijah's cloak that had fallen from him and went back and stood on the bank of the Jordan. He took the cloak that had fallen from Elijah and struck the water with it. 'Where now is the Lord, the God of Elijah?' he asked. When he struck the water, it divided to the right and to the left, and he crossed over." 2 Kings 2:13-14

Choosing the right mentor is important. Do you know how to choose one? Let me help you. Have you ever heard the expression, "Been there, done that, got the t-shirt"? It is self-explanatory. In whatever the conversation is, the person who has been there, done that, and gotten the t-shirt has experienced what is being discussed. That can be a place traveled, an adventure tried, anything. Here's my advice when looking for a mentor: Find someone wearing the metaphorical gospel-sharing t-shirt you want. The reason is because that mentor won't be intimidated for you to "go there, do that, and get your own t-shirt." That's how Elijah was for Elisha. Paul was for Timothy. And, John Weber was for me. Good mentors push you to be all God has for you as a runner of the Gospel Baton.

Baton Carriers: Adoniram and Ann Judson, Charles Finney, Robert Murray M'Cheyne, Elizabeth Prentiss, Charles Spurgeon

CONTEMPLATE

1. Hello, alien. This world, as you know it, is only temporary. How does this reality affect the way you will live your life from this point forward?

2. Where are you a minority? Is it your race? Sex? Age? How have you allowed this minority status to keep you from sharing Jesus, and what will you do about it now?

3. We must be discipled and can benefit from mentors. What's the difference between mentorship and discipleship?

4. Why are mentors so important? Are we to follow a mentor or for the mentor to follow us?

5. If you can't find a mentor around you, what other options do you have?

RESPOND

Throughout this week, ask the Holy Spirit to show you minorities in your cosmoses who are allowing their status to keep them from being all God has for them. Pray for them and speak words of encouragement to them.

APPLY

Do you have a mentor? If so, write down their name and a significant way to show them your appreciation this week. If you don't have one, write down the names of two or three people you know, respect, and want to be like. Contact them and ask them if they would be willing to mentor you. Then follow them if they say yes.

LISTEN

What is the Holy Spirit saying to you?

"Christian mentors do not build a reliance on themselves, but point their protéges to God." –John Maxwell

21

THE 1900s–WANTED: HARVESTERS

> "Then Jesus said to his disciples, 'The harvest is plentiful but the workers are few.'" –Matthew 9:37

Can I state the obvious? The gospel has made its way around the world because people took it there. People left their comfort zones because of a burning passion to fulfill the Great Commission. Many of these people died in the process. Even as recently as the early nineteen hundreds, missionaries would travel overseas with all their belongings, not in suitcase, but a coffin. They knew their decision would cost them their lives. Long before these late missionaries, it was a Jew who brought the gospel to Rome; a Roman who took it to France; a Frenchman who took it to Scandinavia; A Scotsman to Ireland; and a man from Ireland returned back to Scotland to proclaim Jesus. The work is still not over. More workers are needed. Maybe God is calling you?

Baton Carriers: Evan Roberts, C.S. Lewis,
Dietrich Bonhoeffer, Francis Schaeffer, Billy Graham

CONTEMPLATE

1. What is PBA, and do you currently have a case of it? What one word breaks the power of PBA in your life for the advancement of the gospel. (Hint … it's in the title for this book.)

....

....

....

2. Is it possible to make a wrong decision when your purpose of moving or visiting somewhere else is to bring the gospel? What will happen if it is the wrong decision?

....

....

....

3. We talked about what cosmos means in Chapter Four. What does *ethos* mean, and how does it help us to understand who we are to share the gospel to?

....

....

....

4. Under the subtitle "Just Go," where is your mission field?

....

....

....

5. Why do you think few people are willing to go as full-time missionaries to a foreign country?

....

....

....

....

RESPOND

Pray for those on your list from Chapter One to hear the gospel. Also, take a city, region, or country of the world this week and pray for the advancement of the gospel there. Pray for the missionaries in that area who are running with the Gospel Baton.

APPLY

Write down the names of two missionaries or families. If you don't know any personally, ask your local church. Beside each name, write out a couple ways you can encourage them as they are in a foreign land sharing Jesus. Some of these ways can be letters, money, a phone call, or a prayer. Then follow through with the encouragement.

LISTEN

What is the Holy Spirit saying to you?

"The Spirit of Christ is the spirit of missions, and the nearer we get to Him the more intensely missionary we must become." –Henry Martyn

22

THE 2000s–YOU ARE CALLED

> "But we have this treasure in jars of clay to show that this all-surpassing power is from God and not from us." 2 Corinthians 4:7

Almost everyone who first grabs on to the Gospel Baton feels the overwhelming inadequacy to properly run with it in their hands. Afterall, as we've read, this message has been carried on for two thousand years of faithful believers—many of whom are unknown. The weight of responsibility that has been handed to us is great. What's amazing is that God isn't looking for golden jars to put his treasure inside, but available ones. Have you heard the saying that God does not call the qualified, he qualifies the called? That's almost right. There's just one thing missing. God doesn't qualify the called, he qualifies those who answer the call. He looks at our ordinary lives, calls us, and for all who answer, he qualifies us for the task. Will you be one of those who allows God to qualify them?

Baton Carriers: Eugene Peterson, Luis Palau,
Reinhard Bonnke, Steve Hill, Nabeel Qureshi

CONTEMPLATE

1. What is your greatest ability for the advancement of the gospel?

....

....

....

....

2. The book of Revelation is not a horror story, but rather a what?

....

....

....

3. The Bible says that in the end times, there will be an increase of knowledge. How has that proven to be true in the past one hundred years?

....

....

....

4. The last days are here. What is our responsibility with the Gospel Baton in hand?

....

....

....

....

5. At this very moment, the eyes of the Lord are scanning the earth looking for people whose hearts are committed and available to him. What will be your answer when he looks at you?

....

....

....

....

RESPOND

Soon this world, as we know it, will be over. Revelation 15:3 tells of a song we will sing to the King of the ages. Remind yourself of this reality, and focus your attention on the things of eternity and the final advancement of the gospel on the earth.

APPLY

Make a list of things that take your time away from allowing you to be available to God. Which things on that list can be eliminated so you can free up time in your schedule?

....

....

....

....

....

....

....

....

LISTEN

What is the Holy Spirit saying to you?

....

....

....

....

....

....

....

"The soul and eternity of one man is largely dependant on the voice of another." –Unknown

23

TODAY—LET'S GO!

> "Then I heard the voice of the Lord saying, 'Whom shall I send? And who will go for us?' And I said, 'Here am I. Send me!'" Isaiah 6:8

What is seven hundred and fifty thousand miles long, reaches around the earth thirty times, and grows twenty miles longer each day? The answer will shock you. It's the line of people who don't know Christ as their savior. Today, Jesus is still asking the question that has been asked for thousands of years: Whom shall I send, and who will go for us? Notice he did not ask, "Who is the most eloquent speaker that I have created or who is the most charismatic leader on the earth?" The Lord only presented one qualification: Who will go for us? No more excuses. Are you ready to go? The Gospel Baton is now in your hands. This is your moment to ... RUN!

Baton Carriers: Your pastor, your mentor, missionaries, moms, dads, brothers, sisters, the nameless, faceless majority

CONTEMPLATE

1. Do you still have excuses? What are they? What have you learned that can help you overcome these excuses and fulfill God's purpose for your life?

....

....

....

....

2. As a closer, a final runner in this race, what is expected of you? Is this message of the gospel about you—how famous you can be, how many people will like you, etc.?

....

....

....

3. What has it taken to get the Gospel Baton, the message of the gospel, around the world? Who are some of the people who have stood out to you? Perhaps they are cheering you on at this very moment.

....

....

....

4. What was the compliment that was given to David in Acts 13:36? How can that be the same compliment to you?

....

....

....

5. The biggest question of all. This is your moment to run. Will you Go & Tell?

....

....

....

RESPOND

Thank Jesus that he will use you to share his message to those on your list from Chapter One and the countless others who will follow. The Holy Spirit is with you. The Gospel Baton is in your hand.

APPLY

You know that list you wrote in Chapter One? Take the gospel to them. You are ready. Now is the time. This is your moment to run!

LISTEN

What is the Holy Spirit saying to you?

"The opportunity of a lifetime must be seized during the lifetime of the opportunity." –Leonard Ravenhill

ALSO FROM SHAWN ...

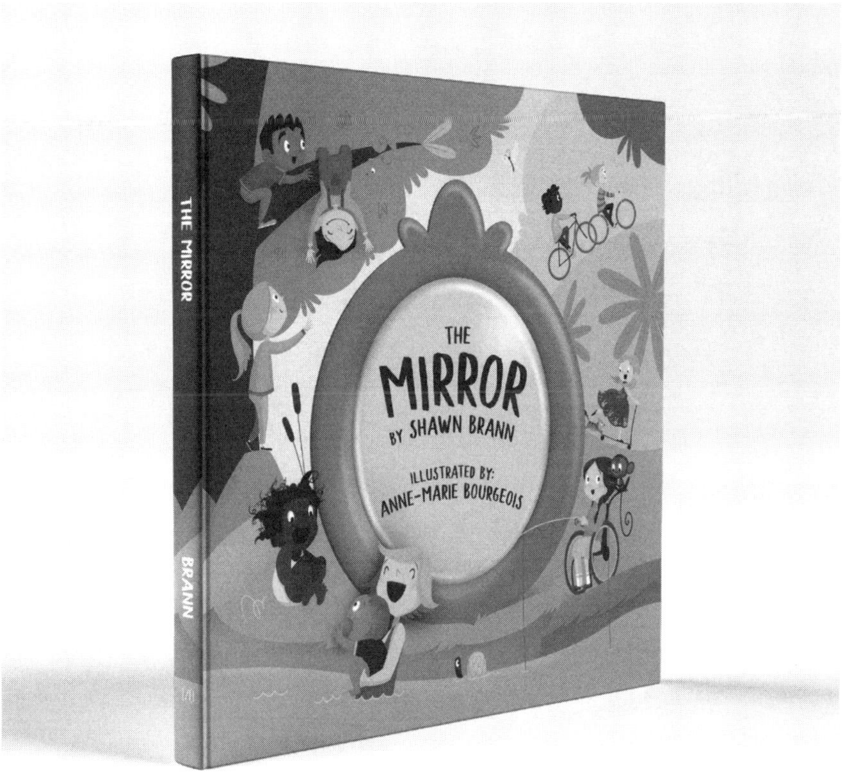

Shawn's best-selling children's book, *The Mirror*, conveys a powerful message that combats the current culture of racism, comparison, bullying, and low self-esteem. It reminds children that God created each of them in his image. And, after God had created all kinds of animals, he wanted to make something more like himself. So, he looked in the mirror and began forming his masterpiece. He would call them people. *The Mirror* gives impressionable little minds the truth that everyone's skin color, personality, and uniqueness are all part of God's perfect creation while celebrating each person's differences.